❖ Golden India ❖

KAMA SUTRA

❖ Golden India ❖
KAMA SUTRA

Selection & Introduction by:

Pramesh Ratnakar

Lustre Press
·
Roli Books

© Lustre Press Pvt. Ltd. 1996

First published by
Lustre Press Pvt. Ltd.
M-75 GK II Market, New Delhi-110048, INDIA
Tel: (011) 644 2271/646 2782/0886/0887
Fax: (011) 646 7185

Printed at Singapore

Conceived & Designed by
Pramod Kapoor
at
Roli Books CAD Centre

Text Selection & Introduction:
Pramesh Ratnakar

Photographs:
Roli Books Picture Library

Illustrations:
A. Z. Ranjit

ISBN: 81-7437-052-8

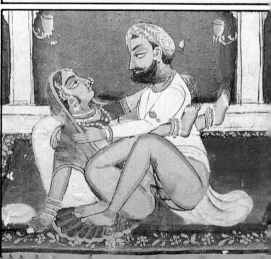

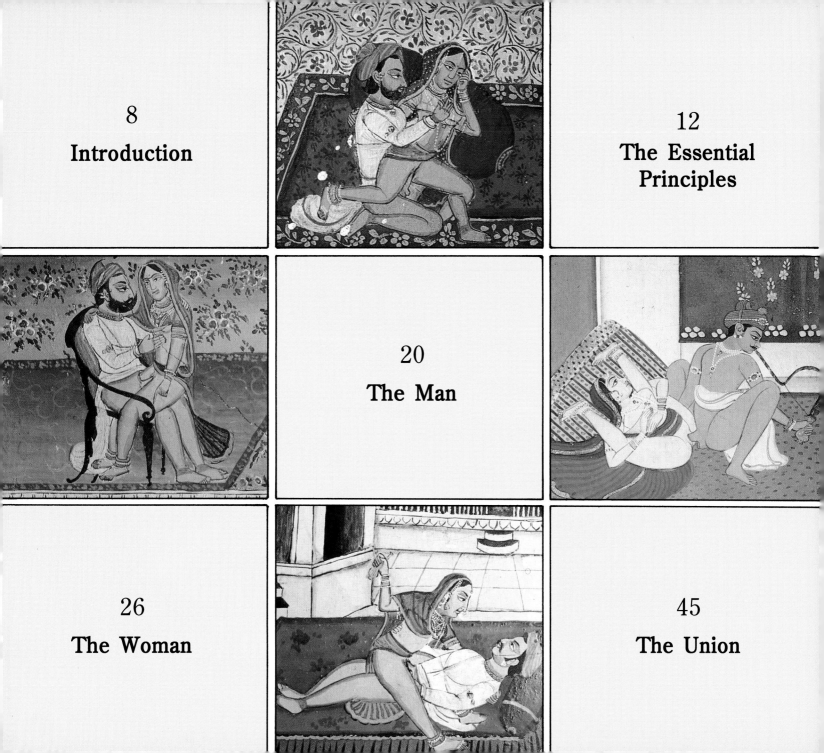

INTRODUCTION

The *Kama Sutra* is widely acknowledged to be one of the masterpieces of world literature. Said to have been written sometime in the 4th century AD, it has continued to fascinate, instruct and

The embrace like 'a mixture of sesame seed with rice'.

delight readers for more than 2,000 years now. On the Indian subcontinent, it has shaped the very current of sexuality, inspiring and influencing poetry, sculpture, music and dance.

The title *Kama Sutra* gives a fair indication of both the form and content of the book. The term 'Kama' essentially means sensual pleasure. Inder Sinha gives a beautiful rendering of the definition of Kama, in his edition of the *Kama Sutra*: 'Kama is the delight of body, mind, soul in exquisite sensation: awakens eyes, nose, tongue, ears and skin, and between sense and the sensed the essence of Kama flowers.'

For the Hindus experiencing Kama in all its perfection constitutes one of the four great goals of human existence, the other three being 'Arth', 'Dharma' and 'Moksha'.

In the Hindu scheme of things three kinds of activities constitute life as it is to be lived in this world: the acquisition of Artha or material goods that provide one with the means of survival; Kama, that is, pleasure, associated generally with sexuality, which ensures reproduction; and Dharma, the ethical rules that define the role of different groups and individuals and enable them to co-exist within the social framework. The fourth aim of life, which presupposes continued existence after death, is called Moksha or liberation.

The uninhibited lovemaking of the divine couple, Radha and Krishna.

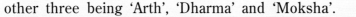

Previous pages 7-8: In ancient India it was assumed that men would play the dominant part while making love. The purushayita postures, where men adopt the submissive role, were considered abnormal.

A girl always shows her love by outward signs, like making his servants do her work.

Without denying the possibility of transmigration or liberation, Vatsyayana, like the materialists, seems to think of it as being too fraught with speculative uncertainty to deserve active consideration. In *Kama Sutra* the author concentrates on the workings of Kama, within the overall framework of life as constituted by the first three aims.

He suggests that the three great goals of life, Kama, Artha, or Dharma must co-exist in perfect harmony in the ideal human acquiring wealth and fulfilling one's are seen to be inextricably linked to practiced to perfection the others existence. Seeking pleasure, religious, moral and social duty each other so that when one is gain as well.

An embrace like the 'twining of a creeper'.

The scope of the book is much exotic sexual practices. Written for original *Kama Sutra* is divided into broader than mere description of the connoisseurs of sensuality, the seven parts.

While one of the chapters deals lovemaking, the others set out to relationships between man and from the furnishing of the house or wooing of the bride and the with the physical aspect of map the entire gamut of woman, covering subjects ranging the planting of the garden to the seduction of other men's wives.

The term 'sutra' refers to the style of composition. The text has been deliberately written in highly condensed versified lines meant to be memorized by students. Some of the other important texts composed in the same style are Panini's treatise on grammar, Kautilya's *Arth Shastra* and Patanjali's book on yoga. The meanings of the terse verses are invariably fleshed out by scholarly commentaries, which tend to reproduce the entire tradition of scholarship related to that particular text, rather than giving a new interpretation of the text.

In the case of the *Kama Sutra* the most important commentary, known as *Jaymangala*, was written by Yashodara in the 12th century AD. It is this commentary which is extensively used to develop the meanings of Vatsyayana's aphorisms.

The love between Radha and Krishna is the ideal prototype of mortal love.

A man should arrange to be seen by a woman on natural occasions in order to befriend her.

9

Apart from what we can get to know from the text itself, not much unfortunately is known about the author of the *Kama Sutra*.

Scholars have deduced from the various references to different kings and queens in the text that Vatsyayana lived sometime in the 4th century AD in Pataliputra. One among the great cities of ancient India located on the banks of the Ganga between Banaras and Calcutta, Pataliputra was the centre of the Mauryan empire. In modern times the city is known as Patna, and it is the capital of the northern state of Bihar.

In the text Vatsyayana tells us that he wrote the *Kama Sutra* while leading the life of an ascetic in the holy city of Banaras. He sees himself more as an editor rather than an original author. According to Vatsyayana, the various texts of Kama Shastra, or the erotic science, were too unwieldy for ready access to the common man. So he undertook to preserve their essence in a summarized form for the general welfare of mankind. The *Kama Sutra* does not claim to be an original work, but projects itself as a summary of all that has been written on the subject before it.

Vatsyayana gives a detailed list of the literature on Kama. According to him the original text was by Brahma, the creator himself, who in one hundred thousand chapters laid down the rules that should regulate human life in regard to Dharma, Artha and Kama. It was Shiva's attendant, Nandi, who wrote the one thousand chapters of the first exclusive work on Kama.

Shvetkatu, son of Uddalaka, is the first human author in the Kama tradition. According to Vatsyayana, he summarized Nandi's work in five hundred chapters. Shvetkatu's name is mentioned in the Brihyat Aranyaka Upanishad and Chandogya Upanishad.

Later the scholar, Babhravya and his disciples summarized Shvetkatu's vast work in one hundred and fifty chapters and later scholars divided Babhravya's work under seven sections and concentrated on developing the ideas in each of the seven sections.

These later scholars who classified Babhravya's work were Charayana, Suvarnanabha, Ghotakmukha, Gonardiya, Gonikaputra, and specially Dattaka, who, with the help of a famous Pataliputra courtesan, composed a work which directly influenced Vatsyayana. Unfortunately none of the texts written before Vatsyayana's *Kama Sutra* have survived.

Although written more than two thousand years ago Vatsyayana's *Kama Sutra* seems remarkably modern in many ways. It disagrees with ancient authorities who argue that the female orgasm does not exist. It insists that lovemaking is the giving of mutual pleasure and that men should think of women's pleasure before their own. It repeatedly asserts that technique is no substitute for passion and that the only rule in lovemaking is that in the final analysis there are no rules and men and women are always free to experiment and find out for themselves what gives them pleasure.

The *Kama Sutra* was first translated into English in 1883 by Sir Richard Burton, the famous explorer and his friend F. F. Arbuthnot. Both were joint founders of the secret underground society known as The Kama Shastra Society of London and Benares, formed with the intention of translating and publishing eastern erotica. It was privately printed and for a long time it circulated among an exclusive set of gentlemen interested in exotic subjects. It was only the upheaval of the sixties that brought the text to the notice of the world. Since then it has gone on to become a popular classic. The present edition is based on the Burton translation.

The *Kama Sutra* is a very important source of information about the life and culture of ancient India. Addressing itself to the needs of the well bred townsman, it describes his lifestyle and his world in great detail. We get to see what he wears, how he lives, what he eats and drinks, how he entertains and interacts with his friends, superiors, family members. Social events like marriages and festivals are described in great detail and authentic insights are provided into the life within the harem, the life of the courtesan and the working of the caste system. Eminent scholars like Basham consider the *Kama Sutra* to be the most important and authentic source of information about life as it was lived by well-to-do young men in ancient India.

To the modern reader the *Kama Sutra* has much to offer. It offers a view of sexuality which is untouched by any sense of guilt, sin or shame. It sees sex as being an act at the very heart of the man-woman relationship and the sexual act itself is seen as the giving and taking of mutual pleasure. Written in the form of a scientific manual, the elaborate classifications given by Vatsysyana and the listing of various techniques of love might seem odd to the modern sensibility, which often equates love with spontaneity. But as Inder Sinha points out, these classifications should be rightly thought of as a grammar of love which needs to be mastered before one can express oneself fully and 'with fluency'.

11

THE ESSENTIAL PRINCIPLES

As the acquisition of every object presupposes at all events some exertion on the part of man, the application of proper means may be said to be the cause of gaining all our ends, and even when a thing is said to be destined, this application is necessary, for a person who does nothing will enjoy no happiness.

Sexual intercourse, being a thing dependent on man and woman, requires the application of proper means by them, and those means are to be learnt from the Kama Shastra or the science of Kama.

Kama is the enjoyment of appropriate objects by the five senses of hearing, feeling,

Women, says Vatsyayana, have tender natures and want tender beginnings.

seeing, tasting, and smelling, assisted by the mind together with the soul. The essential element of this enjoyment is the contact between the organ of sense and its object, and the consciousness of pleasure that arises from that contact. Eroticism is an experience that finds its consummation in itself.

Kama is to be learnt from the *Kama Sutra* (aphorisms on love) and the advice and counsel of men who are experts in the art of pleasure.

A man well versed in the sixty-four divisions of Kama Shastra or the science of the erotic, mentioned by Babharvya, obtains his objects, and enjoys the woman of the first quality. Though he may speak well on other subjects, if he does not know the sixty-four divisions of Kama Shastra, no great respect is paid to him in the assembly of the learned. A man, devoid of other knowledge, but well acquainted with the sixty-four divisions becomes a leader in any society of men and women.

A man skilled in the sixty-four parts is looked upon with love by his own wife, by the wives of others, and by courtesans.

THE THREE GREAT AIMS OF LIFE

During the one hundred years of his lifetime a man should practice Dharma, Artha and Kama in such a manner that they should harmonize and not clash in any way.

Dharma is obedience to the command of the Shastra or the Holy Writ of the Hindus to do certain things and not do other things.

Dharma is learned from Shruti (the Vedas) and from those wise and learned men who are conversant with it.

Artha is the acquisition of the arts, land, gold, cattle, wealth, equipages and friends, within the limits of Dharma. It is also the protection of what is acquired, and the increase of what is protected. Artha should be learnt from the king's officers, and from merchants

who may be versed in the ways of commerce.

It is wrong to think that Kama should not be sought because it is an obstacle to Artha and Dharma. Kama is as necessary for the existence and well being of the body as food, and consequently equally required.

Thus a man practising Dharma, Artha, and Kama enjoys happiness both in this world and in the world to come. The good know this and act without fear.

Any action which is in harmony with the principles of Dharma, Artha, and Kama together, or of any two, or even of one of them, should be performed but an action which harmonizes with one of them but goes against the practices of the remaining two should not be performed.

'NO RULES' IS THE ONLY RULE

The rules of the science of love apply as long as the passion of

man is middling, but when the wheel of love is once set in motion, there is then no Shastra and no order.

It is said that there is fixed order between the embrace, the kiss, and the pressing or scratching with the nails or fingers, but all these things should be done generally before sexual union takes place, while striking and making the various sounds generally takes place at the time of the union. Vatsyayana, however, thinks that anything may take place at any time, for love does not care for time and order.

Such passionate actions and amorous gesticulations or movements, which arise on the spur of the moment, and during sexual intercourse, cannot be denied, and are as irregular as dreams. A horse having once attained the fifth degree of motion goes on with blind speed,

Facing page: A man who is skilled in the sixty-four arts is looked upon with love by his own wife, by the wives of others, and by courtesans.

regardless of pits, ditches, and posts in his way; and in the same manner a loving pair becomes blind with passion in the heat of the congress, and go on with great impetuosity, paying not the least regard to excess. For this reason one who is well acquainted with the science of love, and knowing his own strength as also the tenderness, impetuosity, and strength of the young woman, should act accordingly. The various modes of enjoyment are not for all times or for all persons, but should be used only at the proper time, and in the proper countries and places.

A man should therefore pay regard to the place, to the time, and to the practice which is to be carried out, as also to whether it is agreeable to his nature and to himself, and then he may or may not practice these things according to circumstances. But after all, these things being done secretly, and the mind of the man being fickle, how can it be known what

any person will do at any particular time for any particular purpose?

Vatsyayana, moreover, thinks that in all these things connected with love, everybody should act according to the custom of his country, and his own inclination.

Variety—the Essence of Erotica

The reason for this, Vatsyayana says, is that as variety is necessary in love, so love is to be produced by means of variety. It is on this account that courtesans, who are well acquainted with various ways and means, become so desirable, for if variety is sought in all the arts and amusements, such as archery and others, how much more should it be sought after in the art of love.

An ingenious person should multiply the kinds of congress after the fashion of the different kinds of beasts and of birds. For these different kinds of congress, performed according to the usage of each country, and the liking of each individual, generate love, friendship, and respect in the hearts of woman.

In the forenoon men, having dressed themselves, should go to gardens, accompanied by women and followed by servants.

IT IS TOGETHERNESS THAT COUNTS

A man acting according to the inclination of a girl should try to gain her over so that she may love him and place her confidence in him. A man does not succeed either by implicitly following the inclination of a girl or by wholly opposing her, and he should therefore adopt a middle course. He who knows how to make himself beloved by women, as well as to increase their honour and create confidence in them, becomes an object of their love. But he who neglects a girl, thinking she is bashful, is despised by her as a beast ignorant of the working of the female mind. Moreover, a girl forcibly enjoyed by one who does not understand the heart of girls becomes nervous, uneasy and dejected, and suddenly begins to hate the man who has taken advantage of her; and then, when her love is not understood or returned, she sinks into despondency, and becomes either a hater of mankind altogether or, hating her own man, she has recourse to other men.

Vatsyayana says that the man should begin to win her over, and to create confidence in her. Women being of a tender nature, want tender beginnings, and when they are forcibly approached by men with whom they are but slightly acquainted, they sometimes suddenly become haters of sexual connection, and sometimes even haters of the male sex. The man should therefore approach the girl according to her liking, and should make use of those devices by which he may be able to establish himself more and more in her confidence.

WOMAN—THE ETERNAL MYSTERY

The extent of the love of women is not known, even to those who are the objects of their affection, on account of its subtlety and the natural intelligence of womankind.

Women are hardly ever known in their true light, though they may love men, or become indifferent towards them, may give them delight, or abandon them; or may extract from them all the wealth that they may have.

Ancient authors say that a man should know the disposition, truthfulness, purity and will of a young woman, as also the intensity and weakness of her passions from the form of her body, and from her characteristic marks and signs. But Vatsyayana is of the opinion that the forms of bodies and the characteristic marks or signs are but erring tests of character and that women should be judged by their conduct, by the outward expression of their thoughts and by the movements of their bodies.

Now as a general rule Gonikaputra says that a woman falls in love with every handsome man she sees, and so does every man at the sight of a beautiful woman, but frequently they do not take any further steps owing to various considerations.

In love the following circumstances are peculiar to a woman. She loves without the consideration of right or wrong and does not try to gain over a man simply to gain over some particular purpose. Moreover, when a man first makes up to her she naturally shrinks from him, even though she may be willing to unite herself with him. But when the attempts to gain her are repeated, she at last consents.

THE ART OF SEDUCTION

When a man is endeavouring to seduce one woman, he should not attempt to seduce any other at the same time. But after he has succeeded with the first, and enjoyed her for a considerable time, he can keep her affections by giving her presents that she likes, and then commence making up to another woman.

A wise man having regard to his reputation should not think of seducing a woman who is apprehensive, timid, or not to be trusted, or one who is well guarded or possessed of a father-in-law or mother-in-law.

MAN—DESIRE AND PERFORMANCE

Desire which springs from nature and which is increased by

When a girl becomes marriageable her parents should dress her smartly and place her where she can be seen easily by others.

17

art, and from which all danger is taken away by wisdom, becomes firm and secure. A clever man depending upon his own ability, and observing carefully the ideas and thoughts of women, and removing the causes of their turning away from men, is generally successful with them.

At the first time of sexual union the passion of the male is intense, and his time is short, but in subsequent unions on the same day the reverse of this is the case. With the female, however, it is the contrary, for, at the first time her passion is weak, and her time is long, but on subsequent occasions on the same day her passion is intense and her time short, until her passion is satisfied.

When one of the two lovers forcibly presses one or both the thighs of the other it is called the 'embrace of the thighs'.
Facing page: *In a pleasure room fragrant with perfumes a man and woman can talk suggestively about subjects which may be considered coarse or unmentionable in society.*

19

THE MAN

NECESSARY KNOWLEDGE

Man should study the erotic sciences, the *Kama Shastra* and the arts and sciences subordinate to it, in addition to the study of the arts and sciences contained in Dharma and Artha.

The following are the sixty-four arts to be studied along with the *Kama Sutra*:

1. Vocal music.
2. Instrumental music.
3. Dancing.
4. Dancing, singing, playing instrumental music together.
5. Writing and drawing.
6. Tattooing.
7. Decorating an idol with rice and flowers.

Krishna shown sitting amidst the milkmaids. Krishna's amorous exploits with the milkmaids have inspired painters, poets and writers for centuries.

8. Spreading and arranging flowers on beds or upon the ground.

9. Staining, dyeing, colouring and painting teeth, garments, hair, nails and bodies.

10. Fixing stained glass into the floor.

11. Bed arrangements and spreading out carpets and cushions for reclining.

12. Playing on musical glasses filled with water.

13. Storing and accumulating water in aqueducts, cisterns, and reservoirs.

14. Picture making, trimming and decorating.

15. Stringing of rosaries, necklaces, garlands and wreaths.

16. Binding of turbans, making crests and top knots of flowers.

17. Scenic representation. Stage playing.

18. Art of making ear ornaments.

19. Art of preparing perfumes and odours.

20. Art of dressing, putting on jewels and other adornments.

21. Magic or sorcery.

22. Quickness or dexterity in manual skill.

23. Culinary art, that is, cooking and cookery.

24. Making lemonades, sherbets, drinks.

25. Sewing.

26. Making parrots, flowers, tufts, bunches, bosses, knobs out of yarn or thread.

27. Solution of riddles, enigmas, covert speeches, verbal puzzles and enigmatic questions.

28. The game of starting and finishing verses.

29. Mimicry.

30. Reading, chanting, intoning.

31. The game of pronouncing difficult sounding sentences.

32. Practice with sword, single-stick, quarterstaff, and bow and arrow.

33. Drawing inferences, reasoning or inferring.

34 Carpentry.

35. Architecture.

36. Knowledge of gold and silver coins, jewels and gems.

37. Chemistry and mineralogy

38. Colouring jewels, gems and beads.

39. Knowledge of mines and quarries.

40. Gardening.

41. Art of cockfighting, quail fighting and ram fighting.

42. Art of teaching parrots to speak.

43 Art of applying perfumed ointments to the body and of dressing the hair.

44. Art of understanding writing

in cipher or in code language.

45. The art of speaking.

46. Knowledge of language and of the vernacular dialects.

47. Art of making flower carriages.

48. Art of framing mystical diagrams,

49. Mental exercise like completing the stanza or verse on receiving a part of them.

50. Composing poems.

51. Knowledge of dictionaries and vocabularies.

52. Knowledge of ways of changing and disguising the appearance.

53. Knowledge of changing the appearance of things such as making cotton appear like silk.

Facing page: Vatsyayana says that to win over a woman, a man should first create confidence in her through conversation.

54. Various ways of gambling.

55. Art of obtaining the properties of others by means of Mantras and incantations.

56. Skill in sports.

57. Knowledge of rules of society and how to pay respect and compliments.

58. Knowledge of the art of war, of arms, armies, and so on.

59. Knowledge of gymnastics.

60. Art of knowing the character of man from his features.

61. Knowledge of scanning or constructing verses.

62. Arithmetical recreations

63. Making artificial flowers.

64. Making figures and images in clay.

A man who is versed in these arts, who converses well and is acquainted with the art of gallantry, gains very soon the hearts of women, even though he is acquainted with them for only a short time.

On Getting to Know Her

Now, when a man himself acts in the matter he should first of all make the acquaintance of the woman he loves in the following manner.

First, he should arrange to be seen by the woman either on a natural or on a special opportunity. Second, whenever they do meet, the man should be careful to look at her in such a way as to cause the state of his mind to be known to her.

A conversation having two meanings should be carried on with a child or some other person, apparently having regard to a third person, but really having reference to the woman he loves, and in this way his love should be made manifest under the pretext of referring to others rather than to herself.

He should gradually become well acquainted with her, and he should also make himself agreeable to her relations. As his intimacy with her increases, he should place in her charge some kind of deposit or trust,

The typical house of a citizen with a view of the inner room that is meant exclusively for women.

and take away from it a small portion at a time.

To be able to see her frequently he should arrange that the same goldsmith, the same jeweller, the same basket maker, the same dyer, and the same washerman are employed by the two families. And he should pay her long visits openly under the pretence of being engaged with her on business, and one business should lead to another, so as to keep up the intercourse between them.

Whenever she wants anything, or is in need of money, he should teach her one of the arts, all these being quite within his ability and power.

Now, after a girl has become acquainted with the man as above described, and has manifested her love to him by the various outward signs and by the motions of her body, the man should make every effort to gain her over.

HIS HOUSE AND HIS BEDROOM

Having thus acquired learning, a man, with the wealth that he may have gained by gift, conquest, purchase, deposit or inheritance from his ancestors, should become a householder, and pass the life of a citizen. He should take a house in a city or a village, or in the vicinity of good men, or in a place which is the resort of many persons. This abode should be situated near some water and divided into different compartments for different purposes. It should be surrounded by a garden, and also contain two rooms, an outer and an inner one. The inner room should be occupied by the females, while the outer room, balmy with rich perfumes, should contain a bed, soft, agreeable to the sight, covered with a clean white cloth, low in the middle part, having garlands and bunches of flowers upon it, and a canopy above it, and two pillows, one at the top, another at the bottom. There should be also a sort of couch, and at the head of this a sort of stool, on which should be placed the fragrant ointments for the night, such as flowers, pots containing collyrium and other fragrant substances, things used for perfuming the mouth, and the bark of common citron tree. Near the couch, on the ground, there should be a pot for spitting, a box containing ornaments, and also a lute hanging from a peg made of a tooth of an elephant, a board for drawing, a pot containing perfume, some books, and some garlands of the yellow amaranth flower.

Not far from the couch and on the ground, there should be a round seat, a toy cart, and a board for playing with dice; outside the outer room there should be cages of birds, and a separate place for spinning, carving and such like diversions. In the garden there should be a whirling swing and a common swing, as well as a bower of creepers covered with flowers, in which a raised parterre should be made for sitting.

HIS LIFESTYLE

Spending nights playing with dice. Going out on moonlit nights. Keeping the festive day in honour of spring. Plucking the sprout and fruit of the mango trees. Eating the fibres of lotuses. Eating the tender ears of corn. Picnicking in the forests when the trees get their new foliage. Indulging in Udakakshvedika, or sporting in the water. Decorating each other with the flowers of some trees. Pelting each other with the flowers of the Kadamba tree, and many other sports which may be known to the whole country or may be peculiar to particular parts of it.

These and similar amusements should always be carried on by the citizen. He should converse in company and gratify his friends by his society; and obliging others by his assistance in various matters, he should cause them to assist one another in the same way.

Kama is the enjoyment of appropriate objects by the five senses—hearing, feeling, seeing, tasting and smelling—assisted by the mind and the soul.

25

A woman examining herself in a mirror held by her servant. Vatsyayana advises that women with deformities or illnesses should not be made love to.

THE WOMAN

It is wrong to say that a woman should not be allowed to study the *Kama Sutra*. Even young maids should study it along with its art and sciences, before marriage, and after it they should continue to do so with the consent of their husbands.

A woman should learn the science of Kama, or at least a part of it, by studying its practice from some confidential friend. She should study alone, in private, the sixty-four practices that form a part of the erotic science of Kama.

A courtesan endowed with a good disposition, beauty and other winning qualities, and also versed in the above arts, obtains the name of Ganika, and receives a seat of honour in an assemblage of men. She is, moreover, always respected by the king, praised by learned men, and her favour is sought for by all; she becomes an object of universal regard.

And in the same manner if a wife becomes separated from her husband, and falls into distress, she can support herself easily, even in a foreign country by means of her knowledge of these arts.

EXAMINATION OF THE STATE OF A WOMAN'S MIND

When a man is trying to gain over a woman, he should examine the state of her mind, and act as follows.

If she meets him once, and again comes to meet him better dressed than before, or comes to him in some lonely place, he should be certain that she is capable of being enjoyed by the use of a little force.

A woman who lets a man make up to her, but does not give herself up, even after a long time, should be considered a trifler in love, but owing to the fickleness of the human mind, even such a woman can be conquered by always keeping up a close acquaintanceship with her. When a man makes up to a woman, and she reproaches him with harsh words, she should be abandoned at once.

When a woman reproaches a man, but at the same time acts affectionately towards him, she should be made love to in every way.

A woman who meets a man in lonely places, and puts up with the touch of his foot, but pretends, because of the indecision of her mind, not to be aware of it, should be conquered by patience, and continued efforts.

When a woman gives a man an opportunity, and makes her own love manifest to him, he should proceed to enjoy her.

A man should first get himself introduced to a woman, and then carry on a conversation with her. He should give her hints of his love for her, and if he finds from her replies that she receives these hints favourably, he should then set to gain her over without any fear.

SIGNIFICANT SIGNS

Now, a girl always shows her love by outward signs and actions such as the following: she never looks the man in the face, and becomes abashed when she is looked at by him; under some pretext or the other she shows her limbs to him: she looks secretly at him, though he has gone away from her side; hangs down her head when she is asked some question by him, and answers in indistinct words and unfinished sentences; delights to be in his company for a long time; speaks to her attendants in a peculiar tone with the hope of attracting his attention toward her when she is at a distance from him and does not wish to go from the place where he is; under some pretext or the other, she makes him look at different things, narrates to him tales and stories very slowly so that she may continue conversing with him for a long time; kisses and embraces before him a child sitting in her lap; draws ornamental marks on

27

the foreheads of her female servants; performs sportive and graceful movements when her attendants speak jestingly to her in the presence of her lover; confides in her lover's friends, and respects and obeys them; shows kindness to his servants, and engages them to do her work as if she were their mistress; listens attentively to them when they tell stories about their lover to somebody else; enters his house when induced to do so by the daughter of her nurse, and by her assistance manages to converse and play with him; avoids being seen by her lover when she is not dressed and decorated; gives him by the hand of her female friend her ear ornament, ring or garland of flowers that he may have asked to see; always wears anything that he may have presented to her; becomes dejected when any other bridegroom is mentioned by her parents; and does not mix with those who may be of his party, or who may support his claims.

There are also some verses on the subject, as follows:

A man who has seen and perceived the feelings of the girl toward him, and who has noticed the outward signs and movements by which those feelings are expressed, should do everything in his power to effect a union with her. He should gain over a young girl by childlike sports; a damsel come of age by his skill in the arts, and a girl that loves him, by having recourse to persons in whom she confides.

PUSHING THE MOMENT TO ITS CRISIS

Now, when the girl begins to show her love by outward signs and motions, as described in the last chapter, the lover should try to gain her over entirely by various ways and means, such as the following.

Whenever he sits with her on the same seat or bed he should say to her, 'I have something to say to you in private', and then

when she comes to hear it in a quiet place, he should express his love to her more by manner and signs than by words. When he comes to know the state of her feelings towards him he should pretend to be ill, and should make her come to his house to speak to him. There he should intentionally hold her hand and place it on his eyes and forehead, and under the pretense of preparing some medicine for him he should ask her to do the work for his sake in the following words: 'This work must be done by you, and by nobody else.' When she wants to go away he should let her go with an earnest request to come and see him again. This device of illness should be continued for three days and three nights after this, when she begins coming to see him frequently, he should carry on long conversations with her, for says Ghotakmukha, 'though a

Facing page: A woman on the way to a forest for a secret rendezvous with her lover.

When a woman
shows her fondness
for a man by
outward signs and
motions, then a
man should try
and gain her
over entirely.

man loves a girl ever so much, he never succeeds in winning her without a great deal of talking'.

At last when he knows the state of her feeling by her outward manner and conduct towards him at religious ceremonies, marriage ceremonies, fairs, festivals, theaters, public assemblies, and such like public places, he should begin to enjoy her when she is alone, for Vatsyayana lays it down that women, when resorted to at proper times and proper places do not turn away from their lovers.

The following are the women who are easily gained over:

1. Women who stand at the door of their houses.

2. Women who are always looking out on the street.

3. Women who sit conversing in the neighbour's house.

4. A woman who is always staring at you.

5. A female messenger.

6. A woman who looks sideways at you.

7. A woman whose husband has taken another wife without any just cause.

8. A woman who hates her husband, or who is hated by him.

9. A woman who has nobody to look after her and keep her in check.

10. A woman who has not had any children.

11. A woman whose family or caste is not very well known.

12. A woman whose children are dead.

13. A woman who is very fond of society.

14. A woman who is apparently very affectionate with her husband.

15. The wife of an actor.

16. A widow.

17. A poor woman.

18. A woman fond of enjoyment.

19. The wife of a man with many younger brothers.

20. A vain woman.

21. A woman whose husband is inferior to her in rank or abilities.

22. A woman who is proud of her skill in the arts.

23. A woman disturbed in mind by the folly of her husband.

24. A woman who has been married to a rich man in her infancy, and not liking him when she grows up, desires a man possessing a disposition, talents, and wisdom suitable to her own tastes.

25. A woman who is slighted by her husband without any cause.

26. A woman who is not respected by other women of the same rank or beauty as herself.

27. A woman whose husband is devoted to travelling.

28. The wife of a jeweller.

29. A jealous woman.

30. A covetous woman.

31. An immoral woman.

32. A barren woman.

33. A lazy woman.

34. A cowardly woman.

35. A hump-backed woman.

36. A dwarfish woman.

37. A deformed woman.

38. A vulgar woman.

39. An ill-smelling woman.

40. A sick woman.

41. An old woman.

ON MARRIAGE

Marriage relations should be established neither with superiors nor with inferiors, but with our equals. When a man after marrying a girl has to serve her and her relatives afterwards like a servant, that is known as a high connection, and such a connection is censured by the wise. On the other hand, where a man together with his relatives lords it over his wife, that is called a low connection by the wise.

But when both the man and the woman afford mutual pleasure to each other, and where the relatives on both sides pay respect to one another, such is called a connection in the proper sense of the word. Therefore, a man should contract neither a high connection by which he is obliged to bow down afterwards to his kinsmen, nor a low connection, which is universally reprehended by all.

There are also some verses on the subject, as follows:

A girl who is much sought after should marry the man she likes, and whom she thinks would be obedient to her, and capable of giving her pleasure. But when from the desire of wealth a girl is married by her parents to a rich man without taking into consideration the character or the looks of the bride-groom, or when given to a man who has several wives, she never becomes attached to the man.

A man who is of low mind, who has fallen from his social position, and who is much given to travelling, does not deserve to be married; neither does one who has many wives

The outer room, balmy with perfumes, should contain a bed, soft, agreeable to sight and covered with a clean white cloth.

33

and children, or one who is devoted to sports and gambling, and who comes to his wife only when he likes.

Of all the lovers of a girl he only is her true husband who possesses the qualities that are liked by her, and such a husband enjoys real superiority over her only because he is the husband of love.

Your Wife

A virtuous woman, who has affection for her husband, should act in accordance with his wishes as if he were a divine being, and with his consent should take upon herself the whole care of his family. She should keep the whole house well cleaned, and arrange flowers of various kinds in different parts of it, and make the floor smooth and polished so as to give the whole a neat and becoming appearance. She should surround the house with gardens and place ready in it all the material required for morning, noon and evening sacrifices. Moreover, she should herself revere the sanctuary of the household gods, for, says Gonardiya, 'Nothing so much attracts the heart of a householder to his wife as a careful observance of the things mentioned above.'

As regards meals, she should always consider what her husband likes and dislikes, and what things are good for him and what are injurious to him. When she hears the sound of his footsteps coming home she should at once get up, and be ready to do whatever he may command her.

When going anywhere with her husband she should put on her ornaments, and without his consent she should neither give nor accept invitations, or attend marriages and sacrifices, or sit in the company of female friends or visit the temples of the gods.

In the same way she should always sit down after him, and get up before him, and should never awaken him when he is asleep.

In the event of any misconduct on the part of her husband, she should not blame him excessively though she be a little displeased. She should not use abusive language towards him, but rebuke him with conciliatory words, whether he be in the company of friends or alone. Moreover, she should not be a scold, for, says Gonardiya, 'There is no cause of dislike on the part of a husband so great as this characteristic in a wife.' Lastly, she should avoid bad expressions, sulky looks, speaking aside, standing at the doorway and looking at the passers-by conversing in pleasure groves, and remaining in lonely places for a long time; and finally she should always keep her body, her teeth, her hair and everything belonging to her tidy, sweet, and clean.

During the absence of her husband on a journey, the virtuous woman should wear only her auspicious ornaments, and observe the fasts in honour of the gods. While anxious to hear the news of her husband, she should still look after her household affairs. She should sleep near the elder women of the house and make herself agreeable to them. She should look after and keep in repair the things that are liked by her husband, and continue the works that have been begun by him.

There are some verses on the subject as follows:

The wife whether she be a woman of noble family or a virgin widow remarried or a concubine, should lead a chaste life devoted to her husband, and doing everything for his welfare. Women acting thus acquire Dharma, Artha and Kama, obtain a high position, and generally keep their husband devoted to them.

His Wife

When Kama is practised by men of the four classes, according to the rules of the Holy Writ in lawful marriage, with virgins of their own caste, it then becomes a means of acquiring lawful progeny and good fame and it is not opposed to the customs of this world.

For special reasons and not merely for carnal desire, wives of other men can be resorted to. These special occasions are when a man thinks thus:

This woman is self-willed and has been previously enjoyed by many others besides myself. I may therefore safely resort to her as to a public woman though she belongs to a higher caste than mine, and in so doing I shall not be violating the ordinances of Dharma

Or

This is a twice married woman and has been enjoyed by others before me; there is, therefore, no objection to my resorting to her

Or

This woman has gained the heart of her great and powerful husband, and exercises a mastery over him, who is a friend of my enemy; if, therefore, she becomes united with me she will cause her husband to abandon my enemy

From the very beginning a wife should endeavour to attract the heart of her husband by showing him continually her devotion, her good temper and her wisdom.

Or

This woman will turn the mind of her husband who is very powerful, in my favour, he being at present disaffected

A man acting according to the inclinations of a girl should try to gain her over so that she may love him and place her confidence in him.

toward me, and intent on doing me some harm

Or

By making this woman my friend I shall gain the object of some friend of mine, or shall be able to effect the ruin of some enemy, or shall accomplish some other difficult purpose

Or

By being united with this woman I shall kill her husband, and so obtain his vast riches which I covet

Or

The union with this woman is not attended with any danger, and will bring me wealth, of which, on account of my poverty and inability to support myself, I am very much in need. I shall, therefore, obtain her vast riches in this way without any difficulty

Or

This woman loves me ardently, and knows all my weak points; if therefore I am unwilling to be united with her, she will make my faults public, and thus tarnish my character and reputation

Or

The husband of this woman has violated the chastity of my wives; I shall therefore return that injury by seducing his wives

Or

The woman I love is under the control of this woman. I shall, through the influence of the latter, be able to get at the former

Or

This woman will bring me a maid who possesses wealth and beauty but who is hard to get at, and under the control of another

Or

My enemy is a friend of this woman's husband; I shall therefore cause her to join him, and will thus create an enmity between her husband and him.

A man may resort to the wife of another for the purpose of saving his own life when he perceives that his love for her proceeds from one degree of intensity to another. These degrees are ten in number, and are distinguished by the following marks:

1. Love of the eye.
2. Attachment of the mind.
3. Constant reflection.
4. Destruction of sleep.
5. Emaciation of body.
6. Turning away from the objects of enjoyment.
7. Removal of shame.
8. Madness
9. Fainting
10. Death.

ABOUT THE WOMEN OF THE ROYAL HAREM

The women of the royal harem cannot see or meet any men because of their being strictly guarded, neither do they have their desires satisfied, because their only husband is common to many wives. For this reason, among themselves they give pleasure to each other in various ways as now described.

Having dressed the daughters of their nurses, or their female friends, or their female

If a woman delights in singing, he should entertain her with music and take her to moonlit fairs and festivals.

37

attendants, like men, they accomplish their objects by means of bulbs, roots, and fruits having the form of the Lingam, or they lie down upon the statue of a male figure, in which the Lingam is visible and erect.

Maids preparing a woman for a meeting with her lover.

ON COURTESANS

By having intercourse with men, courtesans obtain sexual pleasure, as well as their own maintenance. Now when a courtesan takes up with a man from love, the action is natural; but when she resorts to him for the purpose of getting money, her action is artificial or forced. Even in this latter case she should conduct herself as if her love were indeed natural, because men repose their confidence in those women who apparently love them.

Now a courtesan should not sacrifice money to her love, because money is the chief thing to be attended to.

When a lover comes to her abode, a courtesan should give him a mixture of betel leaves and betel nut, garlands of flowers and perfumed ointments, and showing her skill in arts, should entertain him with a long conversation. She should also give him some loving presents, and make an exchange of her own things with him, and at the same time show him her skill in sexual enjoyment.

The different kinds of courtesans are:

A bawd.
A female attendant.
An unchaste woman.
A dancing girl.
A female artisan.
A woman who has left her family.
A woman living on her beauty And, finally, a regular courtesan.

All the above kinds of courtesans are acquainted with various kinds of men and should consider the ways of getting money from them, of

Facing page: *When lovers embrace each other in bed so closely that the arms and thighs of one are encircled by the arms and thighs of the other, it is called an embrace like the 'mixture of seasame seed with rice'.*

pleasing them, of separating themselves from them, and of reuniting with them. They should also take into account particular gains and losses, attendant gains and losses, and doubts in accordance with their several considerations.

ON THE SIGNS OF CHANGE IN THE LOVER'S FEELINGS

Now when a courtesan finds that her lover's disposition towards her is changing, she should get possession of all his best things before he becomes aware of her intentions, and allow a supposed creditor to take them away forcibly from her in satisfaction of some pretended debt. After this, if the lover is rich, and has always behaved well towards her, she should ever treat him with respect, but if he is poor and destitute she should get rid of him as if she had never been acquainted with him in any way before.

The means of getting rid of a lover are as follows:

A man should touch her with his hands in various places and gently manipulate various parts of her body.

1. Describing the habits and vices of the lover as disagreeable and censurable, with a sneer of hate on the lip and a stamp of the foot.

2. Speaking on a subject with which he is not acquainted.

3. Showing no admiration for his learning, and passing a censure on it.

4. Putting down his pride.

5. Seeking the company of men who are superior to him in learning and wisdom.

6. Showing disregard for him on all occasions.

7. Censuring men possessed of the same faults as her lover.

8. Expressing dissatisfaction at the ways and means of enjoyment used by him.

9. Not giving him her mouth to kiss.

10. Refusing access to her Jaghana, that is, the part of the body between the navel and the thighs.

11. Showing a dislike for the

wounds made by his nails and teeth.

12. Not pressing close against him at the time when he embraces her.

13. Keeping her limbs without movement at the time of congress.

14. Desiring him to enjoy her when he is fatigued.

15. Laughing at his attachment to her.

16. Not responding to his embraces.

17. Going out visiting when she perceives his desire to enjoy her during the daytime.

18. Misconstruing his words.

19. Looking with side glances at her own attendants, and clapping her hands when he says anything.

20. Interrupting him in the middle of his stories, and beginning to tell other stories herself.

21. Reciting his faults and vices and declaring them to be incurable.

22. Taking care not to look at him when he comes to her.

23. Asking him what cannot be granted.

24. And, after all, finally dismissing him.

A citizen reclining on his luxurious bed waiting for his lady love.

Following pages 42-43: *The love of Lord Krishna and the milkmaid Radha, a favourite theme in Indian painting, is often celebrated as the ideal prototype of all loving relationships.*
Following pages 44-45: *Traditional postures of lovemaking, all requiring a degree of yogic expertise.*

41

The Union

THE IDEAL MATCH

Man is divided into three classes: the Hare man, the Bull man, and the Horse man, according to the size of his Lingam.

Imagination in lovemaking generates love, friendship and respect in the hearts of women.

Woman also, according to the depth of her Yoni, is either a female deer, a mare, or a female elephant.

There are thus three equal unions between persons of corresponding dimensions, and there are six unequal unions when the dimensions do not correspond, or nine in all, as classified in the following table.

In these unequal unions, when the male exceeds the female in point of size, his union with a woman who is immediately next to him in size is called high union, and is of two kinds, while his union with the woman most remote from him in size is called the highest union, and is of one kind only. On the other hand, when the female exceeds the male in point of size, her union with a man immediately next to her in size is called low union, and is of two kinds; while her union with a man most remote from her in size is called the

Equal		
MEN		*WOMEN*
Hare		Deer
Bull		Mare
Horse		Elephant
Unequal		
Hare		Mare
Hare		Elephant
Bull		Deer
Bull		Elephant
Horse		Deer
Horse		Mare

lowest union, and is of one kind only.

In other words, the horse and mare, the bull and deer, form the high union while the horse and deer form the highest union. On the female side, the elephant and bull, the mare and hare, form low union, while the elephant and hare make the lowest unions.

There are then nine kinds of union according to dimensions. Among all these, equal unions are the best; those of the opposites, that is the highest with the lowest, are the worst; and the rest are middling.

There are also nine kinds of union according to the force of passion or carnal desire, as follows:

Equal	
MEN	*WOMEN*
Small	Small
Middling	Middling
Intense	Intense
Small	Middling
Small	Intense
Middling	Small
Middling	Intense
Intense	Small
Intense	Middling

and who cannot bear the warm embraces of the female.

Those who differ in temperament are called men of middling passion, while those of intense passion are full of desire.

Lovers shown to be perfectly balanced while adopting an ingenious posture.

A man is called a man of small passion whose desire at the time of sexual union is not great, whose semen is scanty,

In the same way women are supposed to have the three degrees of feeling as specified above.

47

Lastly, according to time there are three kinds of men and women: the short timed, the moderate timed and the long timed, and of these, as in the previous statements, there are nine kinds of unions.

There are different opinions on the matter but Vatsyayana is of the opinion that the semen of the female falls in the same way as that of the male.

But the consciousness of pleasure in men and women are different. The difference in the ways of working, by which men are the actors and women are the persons acted upon, is owing to the nature of the male and the female.

And from this difference in the ways of working follows the difference in the consciousness of pleasure, for a man thinks, 'This woman is united with me', and a woman thinks, 'I am united with this man.'

Desire which springs from nature can be increased by art.

Men and women have different work to do, but being of the same nature, they feel the same kind of pleasure, and therefore a man should marry such a woman as will love him ever afterwards.

The pleasure of men and women being equal, it follows that in regard to time there are nine kinds of sexual intercourse, in the same way as there are nine kinds according to the force of passion.

At the first time of sexual union the passion of the male is intense, and his time is short, but in subsequent unions on the same day the reverse of this is the case. With the female, however, it is the contrary, for, at the first time her passion is weak, and her time is long, but on subsequent occasions on the same day her passion is intense and her time short, until her passion is satisfied.

ON THE EMBRACE

The embrace which indicates the mutual love of a man and woman who have come together is of four kinds:

1. When a man under some pretext or other goes in front or alongside of a woman and touches her body with his own, it is called the 'touching' embrace.
2. When a woman in a lonely place bends down and 'accidentally' touches a man sitting or standing in front of her with her breasts and he slyly takes hold of them, it is called the 'piercing' embrace.
3. When two lovers rub their bodies against one another it is called the 'rubbing' embrace.
4. When one of them forcibly presses the other's body against the wall or pillar, it is called 'a pressing embrace'.

When lovers meet four kinds of embraces are used:

1. When a woman, clinging to a man as a creeper twines round a tree, bends his head down to hers with the desire of kissing him and looks lovingly towards him, it is called an embrace like the 'twining of a creeper'.

The embrace indicates the mutual love of a man and a woman.

2. When a woman, having placed one of her feet on the foot of her lover, and the other on one of his thighs, passes on her arm round his back, and the other on his shoulders, and wishes as it were to climb up to him in order to have a kiss, it is called an embrace like the 'climbing of a tree'.

3. When lovers lie on the bed and embrace each other so closely that the arms and thighs of one are encircled by the arms and thighs of the other, this is called the embrace like 'the mixture of sesame seed with rice'.

4. When a man and a woman are very much in love with each other, and not thinking of any pain or hurt, embrace

each other as if they were entering into each other's bodies then it is called an embrace like a 'mixture of milk and water'.

The whole subject of embracing is of such nature that men who ask questions about it, or who hear about it, or who talk about it, acquire thereby a desire for enjoyment. Even those embraces which have not been mentioned should be practiced if they are conducive to the increase of love or passion.

ON KISSING

Now with a young girl there are three sorts of kisses:

1. **The nominal kiss:** When a girl touches only the mouth of her lover with her own, but does not herself do anything, it is called the 'nominal kiss'.

2. **The throbbing kiss:** When a girl, setting aside her bashfulness a little, wishes

to touch the lip that is pressed into her mouth, and with that object moves her lower lip, but not the upper one, it is called the 'throbbing kiss'.

3. **The touching kiss:** When a girl touches her lover's lip with her tongue, and having shut her eyes, places her hands on those of her lover, it is called the 'touching kiss'.

Other authors describe four other kinds of kisses:

1. **The straight kiss:** When the lips of two lovers are brought into direct contact with each other, it is called a 'straight kiss'.

2. **The bent kiss:** When the heads of two lovers are bent toward each other, and when so bent, kissing takes place, it is called a 'bent kiss'.

3. **The turned kiss:** When one of them turns up the face of the other by holding the head and chin, and then

51

kissing, it is called a 'turned kiss'.

4. **The pressed kiss:** Lastly, when the lover is pressed with much force, it is called a 'pressed kiss'.

between two fingers, and then after touching it with the tongue, pressing it with great force with the lip.

When a man kisses the upper lip of a woman, while she

the lips of the other bewen his or her own, it is called 'a clasping kiss'. A woman, however, takes this kind of kiss only from a man who has no moustache. And on the occasion of this kiss, if one of them touches the teeth, the tongue, and the palate of the other, with his or her tongue, it is called the 'fighting of the tongue'. In the same way, the pressing of the teeth of the one against the mouth of the other is to be practised.

Kissing is of four kinds: moderate, contracted, pressed, and soft, according to the different parts of the body which are kissed, for different kinds of kisses are appropriate for different parts of the body.

When a woman looks at the face of her lover while he is asleep, and kisses it to show her intention or desire, it is called a 'a kiss that kindles love'.

When a woman kisses her lover while he is engaged in business, or while he is

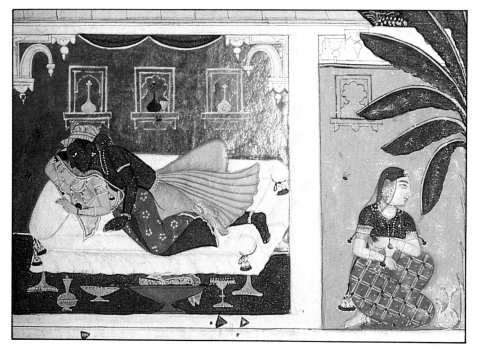

Even those embraces that are not mentioned in the Kama Shastra *should be practised for sexual enjoyment.*

There is also a fifth kind of kiss, called the 'greatly pressed kiss', which is effected by taking hold of the lower lip

in return kisses his lower lip, it is called the 'kiss of the upper lip'.

When one of them takes both

quarreling with her, or while he is looking at something else, so that his mind may be turned away, it is called a 'kiss that turns away'.

When a lover coming home late at night kisses his beloved who is asleep on her bed, in order to show her his desire, it is called a 'kiss that awakens'. On such an occasion a woman may pretend to be asleep at the time of her lover's arrival, so that she may know his intention and obtain respect from him.

When a person kisses the reflection of the person he loves in a mirror, in water, or on a wall, it is called a 'kiss showing the intention'.

When at night at a theater, or in an assembly of men, a man coming up to a woman kisses a finger of her hand if she be standing, or a toe of her foot if she be sitting, or when a woman, shampooing here lover's body, places her face on his thigh or great toe, it is called 'a demonstrative kiss'.

There is also a verse on this subject as follows:

Whatever things may be done by one of the lovers to the other, the same should be returned by

On Pressing or Marking or Scratching with the Nails

When love becomes intense, pressing with nails or scratching

When either of the lovers touches the mouth, the eyes and the forehead of the other, it is called the 'embrace of the forehead'.

the other; that is, if the woman kisses him, he should kiss her in return; if she strikes him, he should also strike her in return.'

the body with them is practised, and it is done on the following occasions: on the first visit; at the time of setting out on a

53

journey; on the return from a journey; at the time when an angry lover is reconciled; and lastly, when the woman is intoxicated.

But pressing with the nails is not a usual thing except with those who are intensely passionate. It is employed, together with biting, by those to whom the practice is agreeable.

Pressing with the nails is of the eight following kinds, according to the forms of the marks which are produced:

1. Sounding
2. Half-moon
3. A circle
4. A line
5. A tiger's nail or claw
6. A peacock's foot
7. The jump of a hare
8. The leaf or a blue lotus

While the woman is engaged in congress the space between the breasts should be struck with the back of the hand.
Preceding pages 54-55: *Lord Krishna with his beloved Radha in idyllic surroundings.*

The places that are to be pressed with the nails are: the armpit, the throat, the breasts, the lips, the Jaghana, or middle parts of the body, and the thighs. But Suvarnanabha is of the opinion that when the impetuosity of passion is excessive, then the places need not be considered.

Marks of the kind other than the above may also be made with the nails, for the ancient authors say that as there are innumerable degrees of skill among men (the practice of this art begin known to all), so there are innumerable ways of making these marks. And as pressing or marking with nails is dependent on them no one can say with certainty how many different kinds of marks with nails do actually exist.

The love of a woman who sees the marks of nails on the private parts of her body, even though they are old and almost worn out, becomes again fresh and new. If there be no marks of nails to remind a person of the passages of love, then love is lessened in the same way as when no union takes place for a long time.

A man also, who carries the marks of nails and teeth on some parts of his body, influences the mind of a woman, even though it be ever so firm. In short, nothing tends to increase love so much as the effects of marking with the nails, and biting.

ON BITING

All the places that can be kissed are also the places that can be bitten, except the upper lip, the interior of the mouth and the eyes. The following are the

In the 'embrace of the Jaghana' a man presses the middle part of the woman's body against his own while the hair of the woman is loose and flowing.

different kinds of biting:

The hidden bite.
The swollen bite.

57

The point.
The line of the points.
The coral and the jewel.
The line of jewels.
The broken cloud.
The biting of the boar.

When a man and woman support themselves on each other's bodies, and there, while standing, engage in congress, it is called the 'supported congress'.

1) The biting which is shown only by the excessive redness of the skin that is bitten, is called the 'hidden orphan'.
2) When the skin is pressed down on both sides, it is called the 'swollen bite'.
3) When a small portion of the skin is bitten with two teeth only, it is called the 'point'.
4) When such small portions of the skin are bitten with all the teeth, it is called the 'line of points'.
5) The biting which is done by bringing together the teeth and the lips is called the 'coral and the jewel'. The lips are the coral, and the teeth are the jewel.
6) When biting is done with all the teeth, it is called the 'line of jewels'.
7) The biting which consists of unequal risings in a circle, and which comes from the space between the teeth, is called the 'broken cloud'. This is impressed on the breasts.
8) The biting which consists of many broad rows of marks near to one another, and with red intervals, is called the 'biting of a boar'. This is impressed on breasts and shoulders; and these two last modes of biting are peculiar to persons of intense passion.

Among the things mentioned above, namely, embracing, kissing, and so on, those which increase passion should be done first, and those which are only for amusements or variety should be done afterwards.

ON THE VARIOUS WAYS OF LYING DOWN AND THE DIFFERENT KINDS OF CONGRESS

When the legs of both the male and the female are stretched straight out over each other, it is called the 'clasping position'. It is of two kinds, the side position and the supine position, according to the way in which they lie down. In the side position the male should invariably lie on his left side, and cause the woman to lie on her right side, and this rule is to be observed in lying down with all kinds of women.

When after congress has begun in the clasping position, the woman presses her lover with her thighs, it is called the 'pressing position'.

When the woman places one of her thighs across the thigh of her lover, it is called the 'twining position'.

When the woman forcibly holds in her Yoni the Lingam after it is in, it is called the 'mare's position'. This is learned by practice only and is chiefly found among the women of the Andhra country.

The above are the different ways of lying down, mentioned by Babhravya. Suvarnanabha, however, gives the following in addition.

When the female raises both of her thighs straight up, it is called the 'rising position'.

When she raises both of her legs, and places them on her lover's shoulders, it is called the 'yawning position'.

When the legs are contracted, and thus held by the lover before his bosom, it is called the 'pressed position'.

With the man's permission, a woman should get on top of her lover to satisfy his curiosity or her own desire for novelty.

of her legs on her lover's shoulder, and stretches the other out and then places the latter on his shoulder, and stretches out the other, and continues to do so alternately, it

When only one of her legs is stretched out, it is called the 'half-pressed position'.

When the woman places one is called the 'splitting of a bamboo'.

When one of her legs is placed on the head, and the

59

other is stretched out, it is called the 'fixing of a nail'. The is learned by practice only.

When both the legs of woman are contracted, and placed on her stomach, it is called the 'crab's position'.

When the thighs are raised and placed one upon the other, it is called the 'packed position'.

When the shanks are placed one upon the other, it is called the 'lotus-like position'.

When the man during the congress turns around and enjoys the woman without leaving her, while she embraces him round the back all the time, it is called the 'turning position', and is learned only by practice.

Thus, says Suvarnanabha, these different ways of lying down, sitting and standing should be practiced in water, because it is easy to do so therein. But Vatsyayana is of the opinion that congress in water is improper, because it is prohibited by the religious law.

Facing page: An ingenious person should multiply the kinds of congress.

When a man and a woman support themselves on each other's bodies, or on a wall or pillar, and thus while standing engage in congress, it is called the 'supported congress'.

When a woman stands on her hands and feet like a quadruped, and her lover mounts her like a bull, it is called the 'congress of the cow'.

When a man supports himself against a wall, and the woman, sitting on his hands joined together and held underneath

her, throws her arms round his neck, and putting her thighs alongside his waist, moves herself by her feet, which are touching the wall against which the man is leaning, it is called

the 'suspended congress'.

When a woman stands on her hands and feet like a quadruped, and her lover mounts her like a

61

bull, it is called the 'congress of a cow'. At this time everything that is ordinarily done on the bosom should be done on the back.

In the same way can be carried on the congress of a dog, the congress of a goat, the congress of a deer, the forcible mounting of an ass, the congress of a cat, the jump of a tiger, the pressing of an elephant, the rubbing of a boar, and the mounting of a horse. And in these cases the characteristics of the different animals should be manifested by acting like them.

When a man enjoys two women at the same time, both of whom love him equally, it is called the 'united congress'.

When a man enjoys many women all together, it is called, the 'congress of a herd of cows'.

In Gramaneri many young men enjoy a woman that may be married to one of them, either one after the other or at the same time. Thus one of them

Cushions are essential requirements for some of the postures described by Vatsyayana.

holds her, another enjoys, a third uses her mouth, a fourth holds her middle part, and this way they go on enjoying her several parts alternately.

The same thing can be done when several men are sitting in company with one courtesan, or when one courtesan is alone with many men. In the same way this can be done by women of a king's harem when they accidentally get hold of a man.

The people in southern countries have also a congress in the anus, that is called the 'lower congress'.

ON VARIOUS MODES OF STRIKING AND ON THE SOUNDS APPROPRIATE TO THEM

Sexual intercourse can be compared to a quarrel, on account of the contrarities of love and its tendency to dispute. The place of striking with passion is the body, and on the body the special places are:

The shoulders
The head
The space between the breasts
The back
The Jaghana, or the middle part of the body.
The sides

Striking is of four kinds:

1. Striking with the back of the hand
2. Striking with the fingers a little contracted
3. Striking with the fist
4. Striking with the open palm of the hand.

On account of its causing pain, striking gives rise to the kissing sound, which is of various kinds, and to the eight kinds of crying:

The sound of *Hin.*
The thundering sound
The cooing sound
The weeping sound
The sound of *Phut*
The sound of *Phat*
The sound of *Sut*
The sound of *Plat*

Besides these there are also words having a meaning, such as 'mother' and those that are expressive of prohibition, sufficiency, desire of liberation, pain or praise, and to which may

When a man and a woman support themselves on each other's bodies, and thus while standing engage in congress, it is called the 'supported congress'.

63

be added sounds like those of the dove, the cuckoo, the green pigeon, the parrot, the bee, the sparrow, the flamingo, the duck, and the quail, which are all occasionally made use of.

There are also two verses on the subject as follows:

> About these things there cannot be either enumeration or any definite rule. Congress having once commenced, passion alone gives birth to all the acts of the parties.

On Women Acting the Part of a Man

When a woman sees that her lover is fatigued by constant congress, without having his desire satisfied, she should with his permission, lay him down upon his back, and give him assistance by acting his part.

Different kinds of congress performed according to the custom in each country and the liking of each individual generate love and respect in women.

64

She may also do this to satisfy the curiosity of her lover, or her own desire of novelty.

The signs of the enjoyment and satisfaction of the woman are as follows: her body relaxes,

When the Lingam is held with the hand and turned all round in the Yoni, it is called churning.

she closes her eyes, she puts aside all bashfulness, and shows increased willingness to unite two organs as closely together as possible. On the other hand, the signs of her want of enjoyment and of failing to be satisfied are as follows: she shakes her hands, she does not let the man get up, feels dejected, bites the man, kicks him and continues to go on moving after the man has finished.

In such cases the man should rub the Yoni of the woman with his hand and fingers (as an elephant rubs anything with his trunk) before engaging in congress, until it is softened, and after that is done he should proceed to put his Lingam into her.

The acts to be done by the man are:

Moving forward
Friction or churning
Piercing
Rubbing
Pressing
Giving a blow

The blow of a boar
The blow of a bull
The sporting of a sparrow

1) When the organs are brought together properly and directly it is called 'moving the organs forward'.
2) When the Lingam is held with the hand, and turned all around in the Yoni, it is called a 'churning'.
3) When the Yoni is lowered, and the upper part of it is struck with the Lingam, it is called 'piercing'.
4) When the same thing is done on the lower part of the Yoni, it is called 'rubbing'.
5) When the Yoni is pressed by the Lingam for a long time it is called 'pressing'.

Following page 66: *When the female puts both her thighs straight up and places them on her lover's shoulders, it is called the 'yawning position'. But when the legs are contracted and held by the lover before his bosom, it is called the 'pressed position'.*
Following page 67: *When she raises her thighs and holds them wide apart and engages in congress, it is called the 'yawning position'.*

65

6) When the Lingam is removed to some distance from the Yoni, and then forcibly strikes it, it is called 'giving a blow'.
7) When only one part of the Yoni is rubbed with the Lingam, it is called the 'blow of the boar'.
8) When both sides of the Yoni are rubbed with the Lingam, it is called the 'blow of the bull'.
9) When the Lingam is in the Yoni, and is moved up and down frequently, and without being taken out, it called the 'sporting of a sparrow'. This takes place at the end of congress.

When a woman acts the part of a man, she has the following things to do in addition to the nine given above:

Facing page: A courtesan's duty is to give the man maximum pleasure. She should be well versed in the Kama Shastra.

The pair of tongs
The top
The swing

1) When the woman holds the Lingam in her Yoni, draws it in, presses it, and keeps it thus in her for a long time, it is called the 'pair of tongs'.
2) When, while engaged in congress, she turns round like a wheel, it is called the 'top'. This is learned by practice only.
3) When, on such an occasion, the man lifts up the middle part of the his body, and the woman turns round her middle part, it is called the 'swing'.

There are also some verses on the subject as follows:

Though woman is reserved, and keeps her feelings concealed, yet when she gets on top of a man, she then shows all her love and desire. A man should gather from the actions of the woman of what disposition she is, and in what way she likes to be enjoyed. A woman during her monthly courses, a woman who has been lately confined, and a fat woman should not be made to act the part of a man.'

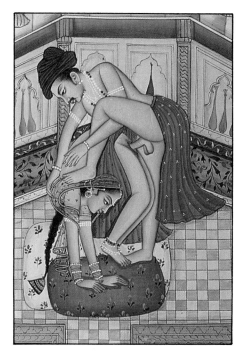

A man should pay regard to the place, time and to the practice which is to be carried out as also whether it is agreeable to his nature and to his partner.

69

ON MOUTH CONGRESS

There are two kinds of eunuchs, those that are disguised as males and those that are disguised as females. Eunuchs disguised as females imitate their dress, speech, gestures, tenderness, timidity, simplicity, softness, and bashfulness. The acts that are done on the Jaghana, or middle parts, of women are done in the mouth of these eunuchs, and this is called Auparishtaka. These eunuchs derive their imaginative pleasure, and their livelihood, from this kind of congress, and they lead the life of courtesans.

Eunuchs disguised as males keep their desires secret, and when they wish to do anything they lead the life of shampooers. Under the pretence of shampooing, a eunuch of this

Young women should study the Kama Sutra *along with its arts and sciences before marriage. This will make their husbands favourable to them, even though they may have thousands of wives besides them.*

kind embraces and draws towards himself the thighs of the man whom he is shampooing, and after this he touches the joints of the thighs and the Jaghana, or central portions of the body. Then, if he finds the Lingam of the man erect he presses it with his hands, and chaffs him for getting into that state. If after this, and after knowing the eunuch's intention, the man does not tell the eunuch to proceed, then the latter does it of his own accord and begins the congress. If however, he is ordered by the man to do it, then he disputes with him, and consents at last, but only with difficulty.

The following eight things are then done by the eunuch one after the other.

The nominal congress
Biting the sides

The congress that takes place between two persons who are attached to one another and which is done according to their own liking is called 'spontaneous congress'.

Pressing outside
Pressing inside
Kissing
Rubbing
Sucking a mango fruit
Swallowing up

At the end of each of these, the eunuch expresses his wish to stop; but when one of them is finished, the man desires him to do another, and after that is done, then the one that follows it, and so on.

1) When, holding the man's Lingam with his hand, and placing it between his lips, the eunuch moves his mouth about, it is called the 'nominal congress'.

2) When covering the end of the Lingam with his fingers collected together like the bud of a plant or flower, the eunuch press the sides of it with his lips, using his teeth

Facing page: *The lovers are shown in an extravagant position with the woman trying for what Vatsyayana calls the 'lifted kiss'.*

also, it is called 'biting the sides'.

3) When being desired to proceed, the eunuch presses the end of the Lingam with his lips closed together, and kisses it as if he were drawing it out, it is called the 'outside pressing'.

4) When being asked to go on,

he puts the Lingam further into his mouth, and presses it with his lips and then takes it out, it is called the 'inside pressing'.

5) When holding the Lingam in his hand, the eunuch kisses it as if he were kissing the lower lip, it is called 'pressing'.

Vatsyayana says that at the start of intercouse the passion of the woman is middling and she cannot bear the vigorous thrusts of her lover, but by degrees her passion increases, until she ceases to think about her body.

73

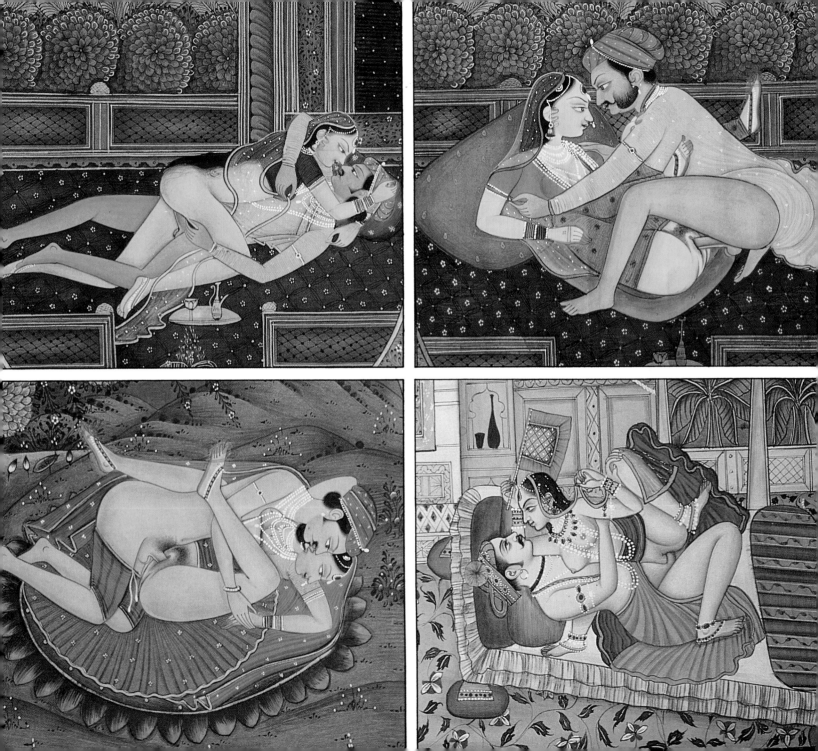

6) When after kissing it, he touches it with his tongue everywhere, and passes his tongues over the end of it, it is called 'rubbing'.

7) When in the same way, he puts half of it inside his mouth, and forcibly kisses and sucks it, this is called 'sucking a mango fruit'.

8) And lastly when with the consent of the man the eunuch puts the whole Lingam into his mouth, and presses it to the very end, as if he were going to swallow it up, it is called 'swallowing up'.

When during intercourse a woman turns like a wheel, it is called the 'top'. This posture is perfected only by practise.

Preceding page 74: *A loving pair becomes blind with passion in the heat of congress, and goes on with great impetuosity, paying not the least regard to excess.*

Preceding page 75: *Such passionate actions or movements which arise on the spur of the moment cannot be defined.*

Striking, scratching and other things may also be done during this kind of congress.

The Auparishtaka is practiced also by unchaste and wanton women, female attendants, and serving maids, that is, those who are not married to anybody, but who live by shampooing.

The Acharyas (ancient and venerable authors) are of the opinion that this Auparishtaka is the work of a dog and of a man because it is a low practice, and opposed to the orders of Holy Writ (Dharam Shastras), and because the man himself suffers by bringing his Lingam into contact with the mouths of eunuchs and women. But Vatsyayana says that the orders of the Holy Writ do not affect those who resort to courtesans, and the law prohibits the practice of the Auparishtaka with married women only. As regards the injury to the male, that can be easily remedied.

There are also the following verses on the subject:

The male servants of some men carry on the mouth congress with their masters. It is also practiced by some citizens, who know each other well, among

A woman, says Vatsyayana, generally keeps her feelings concealed but when she gets on the top of a man, she reveals all her love, passion and desire.

another, and some men do the same thing with women. The way of doing this, kissing the Yoni, should be known from kissing the mouth. When a man and

themselves. Some women of the harem, when they are amorous, do the acts of the mouth on the Yonis of one

woman lie down in an inverted order, with the head of one toward the feet of the other, and carry on

77

this congress, it is called the 'congress of the crow'.

For the sake of such things, courtesans abandon men possessed of good qualities, liberal and clever, and become attached to low persons, such as slaves and elephant drivers. The Auparishtaka, or mouth congress, should never be done by a learned Brahman, by a minister that carries on the business of a state, or by a man of good reputation, because though the practice is allowed by the Shastras, there is no reason why it should be carried on, and need be practiced only in particular cases.

HOW TO BEGIN AND HOW TO END CONGRESS

In the pleasure room, decorated with flowers, and fragrant with

Men and women should occasionally go to gardens and forests on horseback and there they should pass the time in various agreeable diversions.

79

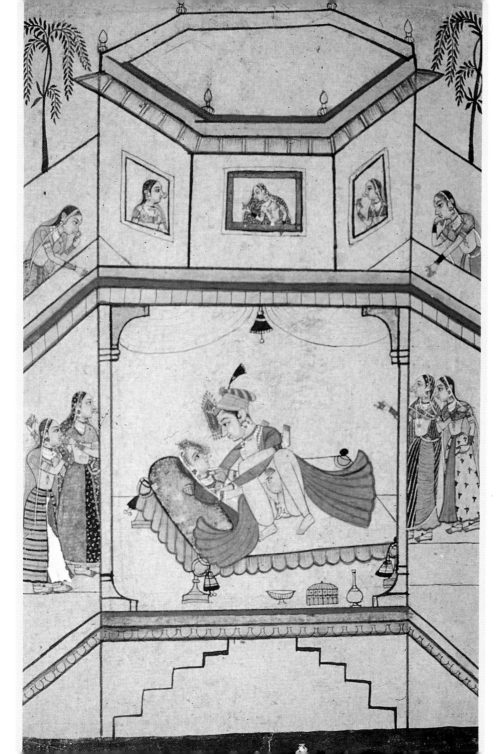

perfumes, attended by his friends and servants, the citizen should receive the woman, who will come bathed and dressed, and will invite her to take refreshments and to drink freely. He should then seat her on his left side, and holding her hair, and touching also the end and knot of her garment, he should gently embrace her with his right arm. They should then carry on an amusing conversation on various subjects, and may also talk suggestively of things which would be considered coarse, or not to be mentioned generally in society. They may then sing, either with or without gesticulations, and play on musical instruments, talk about the arts, and persuade each other to drink. At last, when the woman is overcome with love and desire, the

'Indrani', the posture named after the wife of Indra in which, during lovemaking, the woman doubles up her legs upon her thighs.

citizen should dismiss the people that may be with him, giving them flowers, ointments, and betel leaves, and then when the two are left alone, they should proceed as has been already described in the previous chapters.

Such is the beginning of sexual union. At the end of the congress, the lovers, with modesty, and not looking at each other, should go separately to the washing room. After this, sitting in their own places, they should eat some betel leaves, and the citizen should apply with his own hand to the body of the woman some pure sandalwood ointment, or ointment of some kind. He should then embrace her with his left arm, and with agreeable words should cause her to drink from a cup held in his own hand, or he may give her water to drink. They can then eat sweetmeats, or anything else, according to their liking, and may drink fresh juice, soup, gruel, extracts of meat, sherbet, the juice of mango fruits, the extract of the juice of citron trees mixed with sugar, or anything that may be liked in different countries, and known to be sweet, soft, and pure. The lovers may also sit on the terrace of the palace or house, and enjoy the moonlight, and carry on an agreeable conversation. At this time, too, while the woman lies in his lap, with her face toward the moon, the citizen should show her the different planets, the morning star, the polar star, and the seven Rishis, or Great Bear.

ON THE WAYS OF EXCITING DESIRE

If a man is unable to satisfy a Hastini, or elephant woman, he should have recourse to various means to excite her passion. At the commencement he should rub her Yoni with his hand or fingers, and not begin to have intercourse with her until she becomes excited or experiences pleasure. This is one way of exciting a woman.

Or he may make use of certain Apadravyas, or things which are put on or around the

The Kama Sutra *advises that while making love a man should press those parts of the woman's body which make her turn her gaze.*

81

Lingam to supplement its length or its thickness, so as to fit it into the Yoni. In the opinion of Babhravya, these Apadravyas should be made of gold, silver, copper, iron, ivory, buffalo's horn, various kinds of woods, tin or lead, and should be soft, cool, provocative for sexual vigour, and well fitted to serve the intended purpose. Vatsyayana however, says that they may be made according to the natural liking of each individual.

The following are the different kind of Apadravyas: the 'armlet' (Valaya) should be of the same size as the Lingam, and should have its outer surface made rough with globules; the 'couple' (Sanghati) is formed of two armlets; the 'bracelet' (Chudaka) is made by joining three or more armlets, until they come up to the required length of the Lingam; the single 'bracelet' is

There is more than one way of taking aim.

formed by wrapping a single wire around the Lingam, according to its dimensions; the Kantuka or Jalaka is a tube open at both ends, outwardly rough and studded with soft globules, and made to fit the side of the Yoni, and tied to the waist.

When such a thing cannot be obtained, then a tube made of wood apple, or tubular stalk of the bottle gourd, or a reed made soft with oil and extracts of plants, and tied to the waist with strings may be made use of, as also a row of soft pieces of wood tied together.

The above are the things that can be used in connection with or in place of the Lingam.

A hunter intent on making more than one conquest.
Following page 84: *The female breasts will always remain symbols of sexuality, even though women in many parts of the country were not always required to cover them.*

83